NATURE
BY DESIGN

NATURE
BY DESIGN

Bruce Brooks

Farrar Straus Giroux · New York

In association with Thirteen/WNET

For Alexander

Copyright © 1991 by the Educational Broadcasting Corporation and Bruce Brooks
ALL RIGHTS RESERVED
*Published simultaneously in Canada by HarperCollins*CanadaLtd
Color separations by Imago Publishing, Ltd.
Printed and bound in the United States of America by Horowitz/Rae Book Manufacturers
FIRST EDITION, 1991

Library of Congress Cataloging-in-Publication Data
Brooks, Bruce.
    Nature by design / Bruce Brooks. — 1st ed.
        p.   cm. — (Knowing nature)
    Includes index.
    Summary: Describes functional structures built by such animals as the beaver, termite,
and tailorbird.
    1. Animals—Habitations—Juvenile literature. [1. Animals—Habitations.]   I. Title.
II. Series.
        QL756.B76 1991   591.56'4—dc20   91-15445   CIP   AC

Contents

NATURE BY DESIGN

Animal Craftsmen

One evening, when I was about five, I climbed up a ladder on the outside of a rickety old tobacco barn at sunset. The barn was part of a small farm near the home of a country relative my mother and I visited periodically; though we did not really know the farm's family, I was allowed to roam, poke around, and conduct sudden studies of anything small and harmless. On this evening, as on most of my jaunts, I was not looking for anything; I was simply climbing with an open mind. But as I balanced on the next-to-the-top rung and inhaled the spicy stink of the tobacco drying inside, I *did* find something under the eaves—something very strange.

It appeared to be a kind of gray paper sphere, suspended from the dark planks by a thin stalk, like an apple made of ashes hanging on its stem. I studied it closely in the clear light. I saw that the bottom was a little ragged, and open. I could not tell if it had been torn, or if it had been made that way on purpose—for it was clear to me, as I studied it, that this thing had been *made*. This was no fruit or fungus. Its shape, rough but trim; its intricately colored surface with subtle swirls of gray and tan; and most of all the uncanny adhesiveness with which the perfectly tapered stem stuck against the rotten old pine boards—all of these features gave evidence of some intentional design. The troubling thing was figuring out who had designed it, and why.

I assumed the designer was a human being: someone from the farm, someone wise and skilled in a craft that had so far escaped my curiosity. Even when I saw wasps entering and leaving the thing (during a vigil I kept every evening for two weeks), it did not occur to me that the wasps might have fashioned it for themselves. I assumed it was a man-made "wasp house" placed there expressly for the purpose of attracting a family of wasps, much as the "martin hotel," a giant birdhouse on a pole near the farmhouse, was maintained to shelter migrant purple martins who returned every spring. I didn't ask myself why anyone would want to give wasps a bivouac; it seemed no more odd than attracting birds.

As I grew less wary of the wasps (and they grew less wary of me), and as my confidence on the ladder improved, I moved to the upper rung and peered through the sphere's bottom. I could see that the paper swirled in layers around some secret center the wasps inhabited, and I marveled at the delicate hands of the craftsman who had devised such tiny apertures for their protection.

I left the area in the late summer, and in my imagination I took the strange structure with me. I envisioned unwrapping it, and in the middle finding—what? A tiny room full of bits of wool for sleeping, and countless manufactured pellets of scientifically determined wasp food? A glowing blue jewel that drew the wasps at twilight, and gave them a cool infusion of energy as they clung to it overnight? My most definite idea was that the wasps lived in a small block of fine cedar the craftsman had drilled full of holes, into which they slipped snugly, rather like the bunks aboard submarines in World War II movies.

As it turned out, I got the chance to discover that my idea of the cedar block had not been wrong by much. We visited our relative again in the winter. We arrived at night, but first thing in the morning I made straight for the farm and its barn. The shadows under the eaves were too dense to let me spot the sphere from far off. I stepped on the bottom rung of the ladder—slick with frost—and climbed carefully up. My hands and feet kept slipping, so my eyes stayed on the rung ahead, and it was not until I was secure at the top that I could look up. The sphere was gone.

I was crushed. That object had fascinated me like nothing I had come across in my life; I had even grown to love wasps because of it. I sagged on the ladder and watched my breath eddy around the blank eaves. I'm afraid I pitied myself more than the apparently homeless wasps.

A fine Italian papersmith would be proud to create the colors and patterns whipped up by nest-building wasps.

But then something snapped me out of my sense of loss: I recalled that I had watched the farmer taking in the purple martin hotel every November, after the birds left. From its spruce appearance when he brought it out in March, it was clear he had cleaned it and repainted it and kept it out of the weather. Of course he would do the same thing for *this* house, which was even more fragile. I had never mentioned the wasp dwelling to anyone, but now I decided I would to go the farm, introduce myself, and inquire about it. Perhaps I would even be permitted to handle it, or, best of all, learn how to make one myself.

I scrambled down the ladder, leaping from the third rung and landing in the frosty salad of tobacco leaves and windswept grass that collected at the foot of the barn wall. I looked down and saw that my left boot had, by no more than an inch, just missed crushing the very thing I was rushing off to seek. There, lying dry and separate on the leaves, was the wasp house.

I looked up. Yes, I was standing directly beneath the spot where the sphere had hung—it was a straight fall. I picked up the wasp house, gave it a shake to see if any insects were inside, and, discovering none, took it home.

My awe of the craftsman grew as I unwrapped the layers of the nest. Such beautiful paper! It was much tougher than any I had encountered, and it held a curve (something my experimental paper airplanes never did), but it was very light, too. The secret at the center of the swirl turned out to be a neatly made fan of tiny cells, all of the same size and shape, reminding me of the heart of a sunflower that had lost its seeds to birds. The fan hung from the sphere's ceiling by a stem the thickness of a pencil lead.

The rest of the story is a little embarrassing. More impressed than ever, I decided to pay homage to the creator of this habitable sculpture. I went

Inside the rough outer ball is a faceted jewel of precise cells.

boldly to the farmhouse. The farmer's wife answered my knock. I showed her the nest and asked to speak with the person in the house who had made it. She blinked and frowned. I had to repeat my question twice before she understood what I believed my mission to be; then, with a gentle laugh, she dispelled my illusion about an ingenious old papersmith fond of wasps. The nest, she explained, had been made entirely by the insects themselves, and wasn't that amazing?

Well, of course it was. It still is. I needn't have been so embarrassed—the structures that animals build, and the sense of design they display, *should* always astound us. On my way home from the farmhouse, in my own defense I kept thinking, "But *I* couldn't build anything like this! Nobody could!"

The most natural thing in the world for us to do, when we are confronted with a piece of animal architecture, is to figure out if we could possibly make it or live in it. Who hasn't peered into the dark end of a mysterious hole in the woods and thought, "It must be pretty weird to live in there!" or looked up at a hawk's nest atop a huge sycamore and shuddered at the thought of waking up every morning with nothing but a few twigs preventing a hundred-foot fall. How, we wonder, do those twigs stay together, and withstand the wind so high?

It is a human tendency always to regard animals first in terms of ourselves. Seeing the defensive courage of a mother bear whose cubs are threatened, or the cooperative determination of a string of ants dismantling a stray chunk of cake, we naturally use our own behavior as reference for our empathy. We put ourselves in the same situation and express the animal's action in feelings—and words—that apply to the way people do things.

Sometimes this is useful. But sometimes it is misleading. Attributing human-like intentions to an animal can keep us from looking at the *animal's* sense of itself in its surroundings—its immediate and future needs, its physical and mental capabilities, its genetic instincts. Most animals, for example, use their five senses in ways that human beings cannot possibly understand or express. How can a forty-two-year-old nearsighted biologist have any real idea what a two-week-old barn owl sees in the dark? How can a sixteen-year-old who lives in the Arizona desert identify with the muscular jumps improvised by a waterfall-leaping salmon in Alaska? There's nothing wrong with trying to empathize with an animal, but we shouldn't forget that ultimately animals live *animal* lives.

Animal structures let us have it both ways—we can be struck with a strange wonder, and we can empathize right away, too. Seeing a vast spiderweb, taut and glistening between two bushes, it's easy to think, "I have no idea how that is done; the engineering is awesome." But it is just as easy to imagine climbing across the bright strands, springing from one to the next as if the web were a new Epcot attraction, the Invisible Flying Flexible Space Orb. That a clear artifact of an animal's wits and agility stands right there in front of us—that we can touch it, look at it from different angles, sometimes take it home—inspires our imagination as only a strange reality can. We needn't move into a molehill to experience a life of darkness and digging; our creative wonder takes us down there in a second, without even getting our hands dirty.

But what if we discover some of the mechanics of how the web is made? Once we see how the spider works (or the hummingbird, or the bee), is

Once you start to look, you find animal architecture everywhere: what looked like a pile of leaves turns out to be the nest of a ruffed grouse.

the engineering no longer awesome? This would be too bad: we don't want to lose our sense of wonder just because we gain understanding.

And we certainly do *not* lose it. In fact, seeing how an animal makes its nest or egg case or food storage vaults has the effect of increasing our amazement. The builder's energy, concentration, and athletic adroitness are qualities we can readily admire and envy. Even more startling is the recognition that the animal is working from a precise design in its head, a design that is exactly replicated time after time. This knowledge of architecture—knowing where to build, what materials to use, how to put them together—remains one of the most intriguing mysteries of animal behavior. And the more *we* develop that same knowledge, the more we appreciate the instincts and intelligence of the animals.

Building
from Within

Imagine a carpenter building a house. He is standing on a ladder, putting siding under the point of the roof. He reaches a spot at which the plain planks he has nailed into place require a flat, triangular piece of wood to connect them to each other and the edge of the roof: a complicated piece that needs to be carefully measured and shaped to fit snugly. But instead of going back down the ladder, finding a chunk of wood, drawing the outline of the piece, starting the band saw . . . instead of all of this work, the carpenter rolls his shoulders a couple of times, gives a little grunt, and then pulls the exact piece he needs from a slot between his shoulder blades. He calmly nails the piece into place. Hey—carpentry is a snap!

Indeed, a wood-producing gland beneath the skin would be a great boon to a carpenter, as would a paint gland to the painter, a stone gland to the mason, and a wool gland to the weaver. Humans who build things would save a lot of time and energy if they were able to count on getting their materials from within, the way we now secrete tears and perspiration, or grow fingernails and hair.

Alas, humans have no such interior manufacturing processes. But many

animals do. They are able to skip the often difficult and dangerous search
for materials that other animals must go through before they begin to
build, an effort which drains their energy and time and exposes them to
predators. Instead, these insects, fish, amphibians, birds, spiders, crustaceans, and mollusks make their own materials from the inside out. What
they do with the material ranges from simply using it in the form it takes
upon secretion, to putting pieces together in an elaborate structure.

   The mollusks and crustaceans take the simpler method, and their constructions serve a very simple purpose as well: to protect a soft, boneless
body with a hard housing. Most mollusks and crustaceans live in the sea,
which is full of hungry mouths, harsh currents, and fast-moving food. The
hungry mouths, which would slurp down a fleshy collection of tubes and
tissues, would not mess with a rock-hard shell. The waves and whirlpools
that would toss a soft body against rock and reef couldn't budge a weightier
creature, well anchored in a position that allows it to filter edible matter
from the water flowing by.

*Mollusk shells are secreted by soft tissue called the mantle. These cowries have
extended their mantles over the edge of the shell and onto the rock.*

The scallop (a mollusk) really does have blue eyes! This one also has kelp and a sponge growing on top of it. Like the building that its shape may have inspired, the scallop will sit in one place as long as it can.

So a mollusk such as the oyster—a fleshy collection of tubes and tissues if ever there was one—forms a pair of matched shells around itself after its vulnerable larval stage, when it is still tiny, serving as protection and anchor. It adds to the shells for its entire life, expanding its house as its body grows within. The shells always serve the body. They are held open on a hinge to let the flow of water deliver food, and they are closed with a snap when a fish or crab comes too close. Their inner surface is kept impeccably smooth through the secretion of special nacre that looks like a polished enamel; any rough particles that drift in are ejected or, if they cannot be dislodged, surrounded by the same slick stuff and shaped into a more comfortable roundness. When humans find these spheres, we call them pearls. To the oyster they are nothing so valuable, and are doubtless very irritating even in their perfection.

There are more than 50,000 species of mollusks that secrete shells of calcium carbonate from cells in their mantles (the soft membranes that form the lining of the shell). The chemicals that crystallize into the stony coating are drawn from the mollusk's blood, the water around it, and its food (most mollusks live in water, from which they siphon algae and protozoans). Many of the shells are much more ornate than those of the simple oyster, with flanges, spikes, ridges, and whorls both graceful and grotesque. Some of the shells boast dazzling colors—the colors result from the animals' diet—displayed in arabesque patterns.

The oyster is anchored to a solid object by the left half of its shell, but most mollusks move about, carrying their homes upon their backs as they wriggle along the sea floor, slither across the lawn, burrow into the mud, or jet through the water. Not just the single-shelled animals such as snails and whelks ambulate; among the two-shelled mollusks, some mussels burrow into coral by rotating on the pointed joint of their shells, while others haul themselves onto rocks by secreting sticky threads. Clams dig into the mud by extending a muscular appendage called the foot, and scallops open up and propel themselves high off the ocean floor with jerky spurts of water, to escape predators such as the bottom-hugging starfish.

The most elegant means of locomotion for a shelled animal belongs, appropriately enough, to the one with the most elegant shell: the nautilus of the Pacific Ocean. The nautilus jets through the water by funneling a steady stream from the opening of its elaborately spun shell. This is a nice way to move, but not unique. What makes the nautilus special is the way it precisely controls its buoyancy, and thus moves up and down between levels of the sea with an ease and precision no other shellfish can approach.

In its complex shell, the nautilus animal carries itself up and down and forward and backward with great precision in the water. No wonder Captain Nemo used its name for literature's first submarine.

The secret can be found in the shell: the nautilus builds its home as a series of walled chambers connected by a snorkel-like appendage. If the nautilus wants to cruise up three feet higher, it chemically extracts some gas from the water flowing through its gills, pumps the gas back into a chamber filled until then with water, and then squirts out the displaced fluid to complete the lightening of its load. To drop lower, it squirts water back into the chamber and ejects the displaced gas. This sophisticated shell is secreted by the animal within, just as the simpler oyster's is; the difference between them is as surprising as finding a primitive humanoid living in a cave beside a family in a Victorian mansion.

There are some animals outside the mollusk family that would like very much to have a tough, brittle shell to cover their soft parts, but they lack the interior chemistry to secrete calcium carbonate. In such cases, the animal may secrete whatever substance it can, and construct missing parts

As it grows, the nautilus builds a series of ever larger chambers connected by a tube that carries air and water, so it may adjust its buoyancy in the sea.

with exterior materials. The small larva of the caddis fly lives underwater, where it is a naked, tasty morsel for larger larvae, bugs, and fish. The caddis needs a shell, but cannot produce calcium carbonate; however, it *can* secrete a sticky sort of silk that hardens around assembled bits of sand, stone, shell, and stick, like mortar around bricks. So the caddis larva spins a silk coating around its soft rear parts and scours the bottom for hard materials exactly the right size to press into the silk, chip by chip, to make a cylinder of masonry. The result is a cumbersome but nearly impregnable tube of armor that the larva hauls around as it forages, and into which it retracts its head when attacked.

It is attacked frequently. A predator will pluck up the cylinder and stick its jaws as deep as possible into the open end, but if the caddis has made its armor the right length, the predator won't be able to reach deep enough. It will drop the tough little casing in frustration and go off to hunt another,

The caddis fly larva (below) *has chosen to cover itself with buds and sticks; those on the following page prefer pebbles.*

less-protected prey. Casings of secreted silk studded with tough shards from the environment protect various other invertebrates, from amoebas to bristle worms.

Of course, there are far greater architectural uses of silk spun from glands. Spiders are the master architects of silk, and their webs are unsurpassed in the animal world for all of the qualities we treasure in the greatest products of human design: beauty, the realization in physical form of clever ideas, and efficiency in functions that satisfy real needs.

There are several kinds of spiderweb. The most familiar and fabled is the wheel-shaped orb web, but the others, several of them built by only a few species, also show cunning in their design and inspire fascinating behavior in the spiders that use them.

A spiderweb has one purpose: to catch something (usually an insect) to eat. It can be a net, a pit trap, a lasso, a snare—one spider even uses it the way the gauchos on the Argentine pampas use their bolas, swinging a weighted cord of silk through the air and entwining insects that fly too close to investigate an alluring odor the spider emits. Another catches pedestrians by building a high bridge above a path, perching on it, and suspending sticky threads down to the level of the ground like a beaded curtain. A beetle waddles by and gets snagged on a line, and the spider reels it up like a fisherman. Some webs look like disorderly clumps of cotton with a hole somewhere near the middle; the insect that alights and tries to walk away soon finds itself proceeding step by step in a sticky, sloping spiral toward the hole, and through it—into the spider's lair.

There is nothing bush-league about these various webs of clumps and strings. They work well for the spiders that make them; otherwise, we must assume, the spiders would have evolved something else. But it is perhaps difficult to admire these rather irregular forms of silk-twirling when we have the dazzling symmetry of an orb web before us. Here, we think, is a masterpiece: something we can appreciate with the eye as it sparkles in the light like a jeweled mobile, something we can diagram with a pencil or computer as it sits there emanating mathematical relationships. It is so different from anything *we* could ever do, yet its construction and function are so comprehensible to us; after all, it's probably where we got the idea for catching things in nets, from butterflies to fish.

In so many human processes, we are amazed at a final product but feel less awe when the mechanics are revealed: watching a construction crew put a building together, we find ourselves saying, "Ah, so *that's* all there is to it—those people pound the steel pilings into the ground, those people pour the cement, those people rivet the I-beams . . ." We learn there's no magic to painting a billboard, cutting contact lenses, throwing a curveball. The mystique is dispelled when we see other people—especially with the aid of powerful tools—doing the work.

Not so with animals, and above all with the orb-building spider—who, luckily for us, can be seen at her work from beginning to end in the course of a couple of hours. We can watch her as she stands on a branch of a bush and casts a line into the wind until it sticks to another branch; as she uses that bridge as a base for a rectangular frame; as she crosses it with a thread and finds a central point marked with a button of silk; as she stretches straight spokes outward to the edge, seemingly at random from one side to another, until we realize she is keeping the tension balanced so that an overdeveloped area does not pull an underdeveloped one out of whack; as she then spirals out from the center and lays down an almost invisible series of struts between the spokes, a sort of ghost webbing that she uses as a three-dimensional sketch. She reaches the end, turns around, and retraces her steps, replacing the ghost threads with

A spider sketches its web in a display of midair 3-D, using every leg but one (it, too, will find a job in a second).

thicker, sticky silk. She reaches the center, eats the recyclable silk button, and settles down to wait for something to fly into her new domain. We watch, we see each step, we anticipate the next, but we are more flabbergasted than ever at the toil, the sensibility, and the daring of this small tool-less creature.

In truth, a spider is born with a better set of tools than any human could hope to acquire in a lifetime of browsing through hardware stores. A typical garden spider has a bulbous abdomen full of distinctly separate silk glands that produce six to nine different kinds of the protein substance, which is at least as strong as the much thicker worm-made silk we use in clothing. Some of these glands make dry threads for the spokes of the web and the central resting place; some make a glue used for attaching this dry thread to branches, leaves, or other dry strands. Some glands make threads that are then coated with a different adhesive from other glands, for the sticky webbing between the spokes. There are special glands for the very fine silk used to bind a trapped fly or moth in a truss, and others of the equally fine silk that composes the spider's egg case. All in all, the interior of the spider is a workshop constantly ready to supply whatever material the spider needs for a very specific task—thick cables, thin wires, dry threads, sticky beads—all of it emitted exactly to specifications, without structural flaws.

The spider's physical dexterity matches the brilliance of her material. Spiders set a standard of athleticism in the animal world that Monica Seles and Michael Jordan together couldn't beat. The spider has eight legs that bend like our fingers, with strong joints between segments and feet equipped with combs and hairs that allow the spider to do more than perch on her legs like a table. She can grip, saw, snip, and curry her silk, and she can scamper over her web with speed and stability. There is always a spare leg or two to measure a gap that needs spanning or to spin a recently stung aphid into a storage case until eating time. A spider walking across her web looks like two or three insects joined together in an uncannily well coordinated bit of teamwork; it doesn't seem possible that one animal could have so much equipment working all at once.

By comparison with a silk-spinning, web-springing spider, a honeybee at first glance may seem a pudgy, lethargic sort of insect. Sure it flies, but even in flight it looks stodgy, with its frantic, burdened wings buzzing into invisibility above its inert, horizontal body. It is more a cargo blimp than a swift jet. In a quick one-on-one fight, the spider would surely whip the bee, if it weren't for the bee's fearsome sting. (As it is, most spiders hasten to free bees caught in their webs, cutting the silk around the angry quarry and hoping that it will not return.) Certainly a single bee cannot put forth anything as architecturally fabulous as a spider's orb. But one-on-one comparisons are not the way to assess the building skill of the honeybee, for the honeybee does nothing alone. It is not a solo artist like the web weaver. Put a swarm of bees together, however, and the collective ability in design and construction match the work of a whole forest full of spiders.

Honeybees build walls, as geometrically regular as those humans build of brick; however, the unit of construction in this case is not a solid rectangle of clay but a hollow hexagon of wax. These hexagonal cells will be used, in the rear or higher sections of the nest, to store the honey and pollen bees use to make their food, and elsewhere to house the pupae (bees in a resting stage of metamorphosis between the wormlike larva and the fully limbed adult) of their workers (females who collect food and build) and drones (males who do nothing but breed).

Worker bees secrete the wax from glands in their abdomens; it does not come out in a variety of forms, as does the silk of the spider, but as single, uniform chips that rest in pockets on the bee's belly. The bee slides a chip from a pocket with the tip of a leg that has special bristles, then passes it up to the mandibles (oral appendages that grip and bite like our jaws), where the wax is chewed and mixed with saliva until it is exactly the right consistency to be applied to the cell under construction, adhering to the wax already in place without a trace of joint or seam. The wax with which it blends was almost certainly put there by another bee, and will be followed with a patch from yet another—for these bees build in a cluster, with a unity of intention and appraisal, the very opposite of one spider that looks like several insects doing different things at once. The bees—hundreds or often thousands together—function as a single unit of intelligence and physique.

The clustering of the bee bodies serves several purposes. First, it provides heat, which is needed because wax cannot be secreted or shaped below a temperature of 95° F (it hardens). Second, the cluster provides physical support: bees make bridges of their bodies across the expanse of their walls, allowing those on top to lay and shape the wax. Third, it supplies immediate reinforcements. A bee will do the task before her with an intensity that leads to quick exhaustion; but the second she reaches the limit of her energy, another zips into her place and she retires into the throng to recover and await her turn to resume work. Her next job will be at a different spot, and may involve a different activity—instead of simply laying wax, she may now be required to shave the sides of the cell to the correct thickness with her mandibles, or to measure and adjust the angle of these sides relative to the base.

The wax cell's breadth (5.2 mm in a cell intended for a worker's pupa, 6.2 mm for that of a drone), shape, thickness of wall (0.073 mm), interior gradient (13 degrees from base to lip), upward tilt from the base surface, and magnetic orientation to the earth follow an absolute conformity, maintained by the bees as precisely as if they had plumb bobs, compasses, and as yet uninvented tools for measuring tensile resistance in wax structures. In fact, the bees do possess these things—the worker bee's head doubles as a complex set of measuring devices.

The head of the bee is held by a special pivot joint that allows her to relax her neck and let the force of gravity pull the head one way or another,

The large bee in the center is the queen; the others are the female workers who built the network of six-sided cells.

exactly as if it were a pointed iron plumb bob. Small hairs inside the neck joint register the angle at which the head hangs to the tiniest degree, and give the bee her sense of exact orientation to whatever surface she is using as a reference.

But how does a bee assess the thickness of a cell wall without piercing it and appraising it by eye? Human engineers set up measured plywood molds into which wet cement or foam is injected, so they do not need to measure and adjust the thickness later: the material simply hardens to the molded specifications. But, of course, bees don't build molds—they erect free-standing structures that rise from the base without guidance. Thus the walls must be adjusted as they are built.

Once again, the bee's head is equal to the task. This time the trick is turned by touch: the bee pushes against the flexible wax wall with her

The honeybee's head is like a toolbox.

mandibles, places the tips of her antennae against the indented surface, then retracts the mandibular push. The wall springs back into flatness, pressing against the antennae, which are tipped with special touch-sensitive cells that note exactly the degree of resilience in the wall's spring. We can try roughly the same thing by putting a balloon next to a kickball and pressing each with our fingertips. We can tell that the rubber is thicker on the kickball. Well, the bee's antennae are so sensitive that they can tell precisely how thick the wall is—to within 0.002 millimeter! Once she has assessed the thickness, she shaves off extra wax with her mandibles (now serving as a carpenter's plane) or adds wax, as needed.

Once they are built, the bees' constructions don't lie idly around to be admired for their artistic qualities. Like any great works of architecture from the pyramids to the Washington, D.C., Metro, they testify to the skill of their designers and engineers by being *used*. Worker honeybees are always filling their cells with honey (held in perfectly by the cells' upward tilt), with the inactive pupae, or with pollen, and are always taking these things out. The colony moves in and out of the hive and the cells with a flurry of activity that looks like a speeded-up newsreel of New York City at rush hour. The bees constantly check their structures for leaks that let honey out and chinks that let air in; when a fault appears, it is quickly repaired, with a combination of wax and a substance called propolis, made from sticky resins collected from plants by worker bees.

Other animals secrete wax or silk, though none use them as purely and grandly as the honeybee and the spider. There are other constructive secretions, too. An Indo-Australian cave-dwelling bird called a swiftlet spins its nest entirely out of its uniquely sticky (and plentiful) saliva. Several insects, amphibians, and fish use bubbly foam to encase their eggs: saliva or another glandular fluid is whipped into a lather by the mouth or legs. For example, certain tree frogs in Java construct a small aquarium of foam by leg-whipping a sphere of froth around their eggs as they are laid, and pressing leaves to the outside of the round structure, which hangs in a tree above water. The outer layer of foam hardens snugly against the leaves; the foam on the inside goes flat, becoming a tiny contained lagoon. The tadpoles emerge from their eggs into the sealed "pond," eat the nutrients in their yolk sacs, and wait until a rainstorm dissolves the outer seal of leaves and foam, at which point they dribble down into the true pond above which the sphere was suspended.

From seashell to aquarium, the range of structures produced from homegrown materials shows the hardiness of self-sufficient animals. It takes a lot of metabolic energy to make calcium carbonate or silk or wax or foam inside one's body, and then to create from these gifts a complex structure that will become the center of one's life. More than the strength and determination of the individual species, however, this architecture from within shows the creative efficiency of nature.

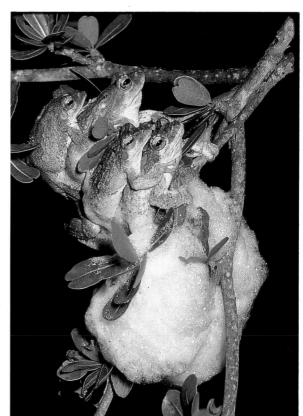

Pairs of tree frogs whip up a sticky home for their future tadpoles.

Holes .

The animals that make their own building materials may seem to represent the simplest ideal of self-sufficiency: they need only their glands, their tools, and a place to build. However, there is another group that takes independence one step further. These are the animals that create structures not by putting up something that did not exist before—that is, not by adding to the environment. Instead, these simple builders make their homes and hiding places by *subtracting*.

Moles and kingfishers and jawfish and rattlesnakes and mud puppies and thousands of other animals—they all create by taking away. Nature gives them the earth, and in some cases tools to move it, and they burrow and bore.

Their art is a secret one. Diggers rule the dark places of the world, and we barely know it. For every bird's nest and spiderweb that we discover on an afternoon walk, we have unwittingly stomped over the ceilings of dozens of dens underground, and leaned against a score of trees housing whole cities beneath the bark. The mound of dirt and leaves upon which we sit to study a scraggly squirrel nest high in a nearby poplar holds a

network of caverns as structurally sophisticated as a fine hotel, with kitch-
ens, nurseries, bathrooms, and underground farms. The squirrel nest we
watch so avidly is just a careless heap of wet leaves and twigs compared
to what a few thousand ants have built four inches beneath the seat of
our pants.

One thing you can say about the earth as a home: it is always close by.
Shrimps at the bottom of the sea find a place to burrow, as do storm petrels
flying in from the ocean. Excavating is something you can do almost
anywhere, and many diggers adapt their simple knack to whatever sort of
soil or wood is at hand. Termites in Brazilian forests dig into rotting tree
stumps; those on the African savanna do their work in sun-baked clay.
There are limits, of course, to adaptability. A desert mouse whose skinny
forepaws are made for flicking sand cannot tunnel blithely into a plain of
rocky volcanic residue. But generally the focus is more on the holes than
on what the holes are to be made in.

*Shrimps and gobies strike up strange partnerships days after birth. The goby needs
a hole to hide in, so the shrimp digs one; the shrimp needs a lookout to spot predators,
so the goby keeps watch. The shrimp always keeps one antenna touching the fish.*

Minimalism: the piping plover scrapes a shallow groove in the sand, tosses around a few shell fragments, and calls it a nest.

The diggers include rugged minimalists, who barely sketch a crude burrow, and finicky artists, who elaborate their holes into baroque edifices with fur-lined chambers and decorated entryways. Even the simple holes, however, tend to be better planned and constructed than they appear. The mice and lizards that seem to be satisfied with a sloppy place to scoot from coyotes or sunlight are nonetheless aware of certain rudimentary facts of life underground: in a hole, you need a place to sleep, a place to store food, a place to leave waste. You usually need a back door. You have to be aware of the level of water underground and stay above it to keep dry (or dig down to it to tap a well). Your tunnels mustn't cave in: if the soil is too sandy to hold its shape around your hollow, you need to dig closer to the surface where the roots of plants bind the soil, or you need to line the collapsible passages with a substance (mud, leaves, silk, saliva, hair, wax) that will hold back the crumble. An instinctive awareness of such elementary rules of engineering guides the work of every digger.

Elementary rules of engineering are about as far as many diggers go in their erudition. Termite mounds and badger sets, as clean and well ordered as they may be, never show evidence of the repeatable unit of construction or geometric layout that we see in the nests of honeybees. Where the garden spider's instinct gives it a blueprint it is compelled to follow, the ant's instinct encourages it to start digging and improvise. One anthill is unlike any other in its layout; indeed, because ant colonies vacate their nests and build new ones periodically (a good reason to call them colonies), we can verify that one anthill is unlike the next one built by the same ants ten yards away!

Is this a sign that animals who dig don't have the wits of those who build? Certainly the mathematically impressive orb web of the spider, with its calculated stresses and spans, and the perfect hollow hexagon of wax built by the honeybee seem to shame the ant nest with its hither-and-thither sprawl of tunnels obviously invented on the spot as if by whimsy.

But we should be careful about concluding that an orderly product is a sign of higher creative intelligence in the individual animal. If anything, the evidence of behavior (as observed by experimenting naturalists) shows that the opposite may be true. The garden spider that builds the gorgeous web will not repair it, even when she takes full stock of a severe cut across its breadth. Instead, she will sit in the middle of something that looks like a bicycle wheel hacked by machetes, waiting for prey to come along, as if her tattered spokes could catch it. After the usual interval of hours or days dictated by her instinct for maintenance (the time varies from species to species), she will tear the whole thing down to build a new one, just as she would if it had not been cut—but she will not fix the rent, though it could be easily done.

The mason bee cannot improvise either. She builds a nice little mud pot, placing pellets of saliva-treated dirt course by course, like a bricklayer, and sculpting them into a seamless, uniform shape. The inside is burnished to the smoothness of enamel and stocked with food for the future hatchling; the egg is hung from a clever trapeze in the roof before the top is cemented on. When six to ten of these are built in one spot, the whole hatchery is covered with an insulating (and camouflaging) mound of mud. But let's find a pot that a bee has only just begun to build. While she's away collecting dirt, let's substitute another mason bee's nearly finished pot. When the first bee returns, she will go right on as if the new pot were her own, at the same just-begun stage. That is, she will keep laying courses of mud until she has satisfied her interior count of what it takes to finish the pot she started, irrelevant though that may be to the substituted pot. She will not notice that the thing she is finishing is almost double its intended height, and misshapen. She will not adjust her compulsion one iota. Unlike the honeybee, who will repair her hive, she is tyrannized by her interior plan; nature has not blessed her with a speck of individual initiative for adapting when circumstances change.

In contrast, the ant that digs higgledy-piggledy is a master of on-the-spot adaptation—or, more properly, the collective consciousness of the entire ant colony is a master. When we look more closely at the skein of tunnels, it is true that we see no pattern. But when we examine a dozen anthills and check out what the ants are doing inside their casually de-signed holes, we see clearly that being free of the compulsion to follow an exact plan has allowed the ant to follow the adventure of more re-sponsive design.

The first thing one notices about an anthill is just that: a hill. Some species of ant build small ones, like individual servings of ocher cottage cheese; others heap up hills the size of sofas, upholstered with leaves or pine needles. The hills are made of soil carried out by the ants as they dig their city; they show roughly the volume of the chambers and passages we could expect to find beneath (though this volume could be assessed only if we found all of the piles humped at all of the exits and entries— sometimes a hundred yards apart—of tunnels connected underground). The mounds are not left overhead just because the immediate vicinity of the exit is the easiest place to dump. The mounds serve a purpose: they catch the sunlight and collect warmth, which passes downward. Despite the usefulness of the mound, however, the ants do not begin piling up dirt as soon as they start to dig a new nest—at the beginning, in fact, they go to great pains to carry it away from the entry and hide it. A new nest is a simple, short hole, and ants working in it could be easily rooted out by a hungry predator who noticed the telltale pile. So the mounds do not appear until the diggers feel secure in the twists and turns of the galleries below.

Ants appear to like crisply defined things: their society is a system of castes, in which the divisions are marked absolutely by body type, gender, and type of work. So it is within their nests: each chamber has its purpose. In this one the queen is tended, in that one the eggs; in these twenty near the surface are sealed the feces of the whole population, carted off by workers functioning as sanitation engineers. It is in the chambers reserved for food storage that the most surprising behavior of ants is revealed.

It took entomologists—scientists who study insects—a long time to figure out how several kinds of ants fed themselves, despite the fact that ants are pretty much an open book for observation. An observer can slice open a nest and watch the ants inside continue working as if he or she weren't there, or follow them and note every phase of their expeditions. Ants are the most self-confident of animals: they know what they have to do, and they do it without fear or suspiciousness. If someone wants to watch, fine; if the watcher rips up a few tunnels, it's a nuisance, but they'll be repaired.

So scientists could always see ants doing strange things—one species carrying aphids around from one plant to another, for example, or another species cutting circular disks out of leaves and carrying them underground. They just couldn't figure out what the point was.

They couldn't figure it out largely because the ants' cultivation of food sources was so sophisticated that no one wanted to come right out in the scientific community and say, "Hey, I've got it: some ants raise livestock, some maintain granaries, and some cultivate underground gardens!" Yet that is what different ant species do, and scientists finally came to realize it.

We can find chambers of an ant nest filled with aphids sucking on carefully exposed underground roots, and other rooms filled with aphid eggs, because quite a few species of ant live on the honeydew that aphids manufacture from plant juices. Ants tend entire herds of aphids just as responsibly as human farmers tend their dairy cows, carrying the smaller bugs to greener pastures when they have overgrazed a plant, breeding them, and milking them (an aphid secretes large drops of honeydew when an ant—whose special job it is—caresses it with a very delicate tickling procedure; the ant laps up the honeydew and regurgitates it to share with others). Despite the evidence within the architecture, who would have thought ants raised livestock? For a long time scientists thought the ants just had an aphid problem, like a human gardener scowling at his infested roses.

Other scientists, who had watched long lines of a different species of ant cutting circular disks out of leaves and carrying the disks by the hundreds underground, dug up chambers in which these leaves lay covered with a moldy fungus and concluded that ant nests were pitifully afflicted by resilient strains of mildew. Why the ants carried the leaves underground and stockpiled them in the first place was a mystery, but the presence of the mold was not: stray spores had crept in and ruined the leaves, said the experts. They determined that the fungus was a kind they found no-

These Texas carpenter ants are tending their herd of aphids as carefully as any cowboy watching his longhorn cattle. Notice how the rear segments of several ants bulge with honeydew extracted from the aphids.

where else in nature, but this was viewed as a mildly interesting accident.

It was a long time before someone finally noticed that whenever these ants built a new nest, or set up a new queen to start a colony of her own, the first thing they installed was a culture of the mystery fungus ("Hey—they seem to *want* the stuff!"). Then someone discovered that the leaf disks received a great deal of careful treatment before they were taken underground: they were moistened or dried, depending on their relative condition. Next they were chewed into a spongy mass, carefully laid out in large rooms, and—could it be?—allowed, even *encouraged* (with fecal fertilizer, like that used by our mushroom farmers), to become the host for the fungus. And once the fungus began to grow, a caste of gardener ants kept a close watch on it, rigorously weeding out all other kinds of growth and keeping the original fungus pure. At last one British experi-

Leaf-cutting ants marching home with their compost.

menter took the plunge, publishing a scientific paper in 1874 to avow that the ants *ate* the fungus; in fact, they ate nothing else. The collection and preparation of the leaves, the isolation in dark chambers, the vigilant weeding—all of this was just a sophisticated process of food production. The scientist was ridiculed for twenty years. But eventually his thesis was proved correct.

In other parts of the animal world, the rabbit warrens and badger sets and fox dens do not demonstrate such a creative specificity as the ant colonies, but they do tend to resemble the ant nests in being sprawling networks of well-dug passages and rooms supporting a collective society, whether small or large. Mostly, the burrowing mammals, birds, and reptiles of desert and woodland use their subterranean apartments for sleeping and nurturing their offspring through their most vulnerable months (much as aquatic mammals use bodies of water). Like most ants, they are essentially above-ground dwellers who happen to have found a safer niche below. In addition, these animals are not physically much different from

Bank swallows and the ancient Anasazi people of the American Southwest chose to build high and dry in desert cliffs.

The fennec fox digs a cool burrow in the desert, with plenty of room for those ears.

Sometimes you'd be surprised by what might pop
out of a hole in the ground.

non-burrowers, and they are still quite comfortable seeking their food out in the open.

But, of course, there *is* one animal obviously endowed just for digging, and it is not especially comfortable out in the wide world: the mole. Moles are nearly blind; they have huge, heavy-nailed front paws turned sideways, making it much easier to lie flat and dig than to stand and walk; their snouts are covered with unique sensory organs that science has yet to figure out—they apparently combine hypersensitive touch with something between taste and smell; their favorite food is the earthworm; and they cannot tolerate company. In other words, a mole is perfectly equipped for a life of digging dark tunnels and roaming them alone.

When food below runs short and the ground freezes too hard for much digging, a mole will surface (usually at night) and poke around for something to eat, but it much prefers to stay in its catacombs and grab worms and insects, digging below the frost level when winter comes. Moles are born below and inherit the tunnels of their forebears, and a young mole may never dig a spadeful if its fiefdom remains intact and well stocked

Mole tunnels.

with food. But when a tunnel collapses or the worms stay away, the digging starts. The mole is not just restless: its tunnels serve as traps for the invertebrates it eats, so by extending its holes it is casting a wider net. When the hunting is good, a mole stockpiles food in a central chamber, immobilizing but not killing worms by biting off end segments that contain nerve centers controlling the ability to move. In one such larder a student of mole life counted almost thirteen hundred neatly nipped earthworms.

Moles ventilate their holes by burrowing up to daylight at strategic points around their domain; such poke-throughs make what we call molehills. Larger piles of dirt may indicate that a mole has just repaired a collapsed passage. No one knows why a mole digs in one place rather than another, largely because we don't know just what their strangely arrayed senses tell them. One European mole tunneled exactly beneath the white lines of a clay tennis court, possibly because it anticipated some beneficial effect (on the soil? on the worms?) from the lime stripes above.

It may seem like stretching the term to call moles and ants and badgers and digger wasps "architects," because we associate that word with solid structures revealing a regular design. But no animals, with the exception of the shellfish that live entirely within their homemade coatings, depend more on their designs, however rough, to contain their lives.

Building from the Environment

Before humans invented such chemical artificialities as fiberglass and polyurethane, there wasn't much difference between our building materials and those of animals. In most cases, there wasn't even much difference between the basic techniques for using the clay and mud, wood and pulp, grass, straw, leaf, stone, ice, sand, cotton, and wool. Sometimes we have swiped a good technical idea from an animal. Wasps probably showed us how to make paper, spiders how to make nets. Birds' nests may have inspired the first crafter of baskets. One type of ovenbird found in Brazil, which builds a staunch, crack-free nest of clay mud, showed scientists in the 1950s a secret ingredient (dung) that improved the adobe of which human dwellings were being made—which in turn quashed an epidemic of deadly blood disease carried by biting bugs that bred in the cracks common to the *human* walls.

Structures for animals are not a matter of pure aesthetics, or even comfort. Staying out of an ice storm, insulating an egg, hiding from a killer, winning a mate, storing food—these are matters of life and death for every species that builds something. Nevertheless, comfort and beauty often

The adobe concocted by the ovenbird for its nest proved to be superior to human adobe—so the bird's recipe was adopted for human buildings.

serve the goal of survival. The exuberant artistry of male bowerbirds produces objects that exist only to be visually impressive: they do not shelter, they do not trap prey, no one lays eggs in them. The bird that builds them is guided entirely by his sense of what will be beautiful to a female of his species. He erects a fabulous pavilion or tower of reeds and grass, then decorates it lavishly with flowers, buds, bones, bottle caps, cones, yarn, shells from snails, or shotgun ammo—almost anything brightly colored and portable. The satin bowerbird even mixes a paint of berry juice and daubs it on his bower walls with a brush of teased-out bark held in his beak.

Aren't these rococo things products of "pure aesthetics"? How are they different from a mobile made by Calder, or the Watts Towers? What do they have to do with survival?

We must remember that for an animal, the drive to reproduce the species is a key element in the compulsion to survive as an individual. Raising offspring is as urgent as eating. In most species, it is the responsibility of the male to secure a female mate through the performance of rituals that do not always have any biologically reproductive function; often, these rituals require nothing more than a kind of showing off. The females watch (and sometimes join in) as the males strut or sing or flash bright fur or horns or feathers. Then they bestow their approval on a particularly impressive suitor, and a new family is made. For the male bowerbird the compulsive ritual is building fancy sculptures so that its species may survive.

Birds whose mating ritual is one of song or athleticism, rather than architecture, are more utilitarian in their building. Once they have found mates, they build not bowers but nests, for laying eggs in. The first weeks of spring (breeding season for the birds we see in North America) reveal a frenzy of construction to anyone who takes a pair of binoculars and sits

The male satin bowerbird (right) *watches hopefully as the female checks out his ritualized construction.*

in woods whose trees haven't sprouted leaves yet. Birds dart around picking up bits of appropriate material and flying back to pack it all into a tangle that will become a nest. Except for the swiftlets that make nests of their own saliva, nest-building birds use exterior materials. (Several humming-birds make nests primarily of silk, but they don't spin it. They steal it from spiders.) Some nests are made entirely from a single substance; others may contain thirty to forty different materials. A species may rely on a strict recipe passed on by instinct from generation to generation, flying great distances to find a particular material. Others improvise every year, depending on what is available nearby, substituting to make the job easy. The "horsehair bird," so called because it used to rely on strands plucked from the tails of horses to bind its nest, should now be called the mono-filament bird: as horses were replaced by tailless automobiles and game fishing grew as a pastime, the bird began picking up snarls of fishing line to replace the increasingly scarce natural fiber.

Holding a bird's nest in our hands gave many of us our first awed realization that there was more going on in the animal world than we reckoned. Probably we liked wild animals, but we had been taught they were pretty crude and simpleminded—fun to watch in zoos or woods, great characters for cartoons and books, but not exactly on the ball. But when we shinnied a tree during the winter and plucked a lapidary little basket from a branch, we were stunned at the non-human perfection of it, and we asked: If animals are so inferior, how come they can make *this*?

Birds' nests as relics of structural ingenuity can be more impressive than scallop shells, spiderwebs, anthills, and honeycombs, for a lot of reasons. First is the fact that they are so obviously handmade. Compared to a cup of woven reeds lined with milkweed down and covered with moss, a sea-shell may seem cold, detached, merely oozed without consciousness; so may a wax wall of perfect hexagons, constructed in a fanatical focus that is just *too* neat. Second, this handmade quality is especially amazing be-cause birds have no arms or hands. Spiders have eight legs and ants six—so we can almost expect them to produce marvels. But birds have two twiggy feet and a beak. To weave leaves or mold clay with that limited equipment strikes us as heroic.

Weaving is among the greatest of the bird's feats. Quite a few birds do it, with varying degrees of intricacy. The finest craftsmen may be the well-named weaverbirds of Africa and Asia. Using grasses, strips of bark, reeds, twigs, or strands of plant silk, a male weaverbird can plait and splice and purl, and he knows how to make half a dozen kinds of knot as well. The

In some parts of Alaska, moss and lichen are easier to find than grass, so the golden plover makes them the main material of its nest.

males, like the bowerbirds, build to attract females, but the nests are actually used. Once a female has accepted the nest and laid eggs, the male leaves to build another, establishing a second family, and then a third, and so on. Interestingly, young males who are not yet ready to mate begin building nests anyway. The nests are too rough to draw any notice from females who can pick the offerings of older, more accomplished artists. But the birds gain experience from this practice, and their nests get better as they experiment with new techniques. When they reach maturity, they have acquired the handiness to compete.

If there is a bird that can weave, is there also one that can sew? Certainly. The tailorbird of Asia creates a nest for itself from a large, living leaf. The bird wants to turn the flat leaf into a sort of bag that will hold a nest lined with plant down and soft fibers, protecting it, insulating it, and—because the nest is essentially grafted onto a growing part of a healthy plant—

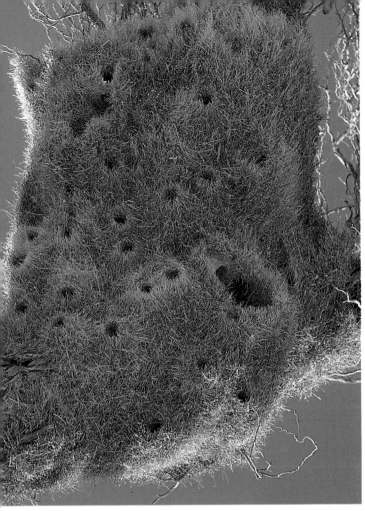

The sociable weavers erect cities of straw, housing hundreds, and cliff swallows build mud huts on blocks of rock.

A ruby-throated hummingbird (left) in Ohio uses moss and lichen for the final touch of decor on a nest made mainly of spider silk.

obscuring it from view. To make this sac, the tailorbird uses its bill to puncture the edges of the leaf with a series of regular holes. Then, with threads of silk picked from webs and cocoons, or strands of bark peeled from trees, or tufts of cotton rolled into string, the bird pushes stitches through the holes with its bill, tying knots to hold the thread ends in place, and eventually pulling the sides of the leaf into the tucked shape it needs.

Leaves are also the raw material for the nest of the weaver ant, but the ants do not pierce the leaf with holes and stitch through them, nor do they really weave. Their process of construction is perhaps more athletic than refined, but its resourcefulness is amazing. Usually between a hundred and five hundred of these ants select a living leaf, and, working with coordinated strength, pull two of its edges together. The leaf naturally tends to spring against such a bend, to resume its flat shape, but the ants keep it doubled up with a typically valiant maneuver: individual ants grasp the two edges that will be joined, and hold them together, using their bodies as sutures. (This is quite a feat, something like folding a very large mattress in two and holding it that way, one edge with your teeth and the other with your feet.)

Weaver ants! Some pull the leaf's edges together so that others can stitch the gap closed, by pressing silk from the white larvae held in their jaws.

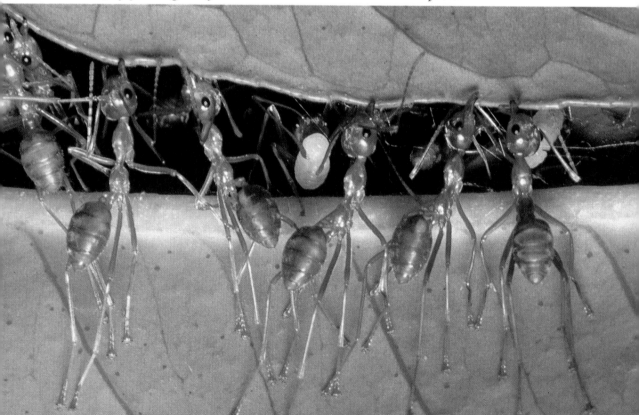

While they hold the edges together, other ants rush onto the scene with a surprising sort of tool held out in their jaws: wormlike larvae from the colony's nursery. These larvae have the ability to spin silk cocoons for themselves. It is this silk the adults are after, and they feel no qualms about putting the squeeze on their young for a contribution. The adult shoves the mouth of the larva against one edge of the leaf until the silk starts to flow; then it carries the larva to the other side, spanning the gap with a taut strand as it is secreted. A second push, on the second edge, fastens the "stitch," and the larva is shuttled back across the gap, leaving another strand in place. Eventually a tapestry of silk fixes permanently what the bridging bodies held at first, and the drained larvae are carried back to their nurseries, at least until they are needed again to repair a rip in the tapestry. Most of the larvae will never actually make cocoons for themselves—they haven't enough silk left to spin—and they survive anyway. Apparently, they don't actually *need* cocoons, but keep their silk for this construction purpose.

Though these nests are built directly into the life of the host plant, they don't usually obstruct its growth. Most nests are relatively unobtrusive: they sit on the periphery of a particular environment's normal functioning, staying out of the way of nature's momentum as much as possible. But one creature—perhaps the best known of all animal builders—makes a point of obstructing.

The beaver lives in a series of dry chambers with an underwater entrance. Where a big, deep river with a steady flow provides a stable water level, beavers may simply dig a burrow into the riverbank. But in places where the river is not deep enough or even enough in its flow, these large aquatic rodents prefer to build a heaping mound of wood and mud called a lodge. Working together, the male and female (who mate for life) start from the bottom underwater, laying a foundation of tree limbs and rocks. They chop down the trees they need—or, rather, they gnaw them down with their blade-like front teeth, cutting circular grooves around the trunk until the tree tilts and falls. They trim the limbs from the trunk, carry the branches away for future construction use (or for eating: beavers live largely on bark and leaves), then either drag the limbs to the river's edge along carefully tended paths, or float them through carefully dug canals. Limbs that will be used for the lodge foundation are usually subjected to the process of waterlogging (sometimes being held underwater by large rocks), so that they will not float out of place when they are laid in the underwater foundation.

The lodge is built upward, all twigs and bark with mud caulking. It becomes a handmade island, sticking up from the middle of the water. But its passageways—which lead to the living chambers—must have underwater entrances that can be reached only by an expert swimmer; if the stream is too shallow, any animal could wade to the holes and wander in. In such cases, therefore, the beavers must first make their artificial island respectable by surrounding it with an artificial lake.

The beavers have a water source to fill their lake: the stream or river that flows by, in all its regrettable shallowness and hurry. What they need is to slow down the flow and back the stream up so that the water collects into a quieter, deeper pool. So, downstream from the site of their lodge, they build a dam.

A dam is nothing but a wall that stands in the way of water. A wall is a pretty simple structure, but when a strong stream is going to be constantly pushing against it, the engineering requirements grow rigorous. The beavers are equal to the task. Working in the surge of the current they hope to stop, they lay a strong foundation of large branches, braced on the downstream side by poles jammed into the stream bottom or banks, and by forked limbs set against sturdy trees. From this base the wall rises, layer upon layer of branches and twigs and chips and bark, all forced into a compact, watertight structure reinforced with heavy rocks and sealed with mud. The mud and some of the stones come from a kind of quarry dug in the bottom just on the upstream side of the dam. This pit has an important function, too: it slows down the force of the current just before the water hits the dam.

A beaver dam is not an inflexible edifice; it is an adjustable tool. Once the stream has backed up and collected into a still pond, and the lodge has been built, the beavers can regulate the depth of the water by cutting spillways into the top of the dam (to lower the level of the pool). Monitoring the water level and maintaining the dam are big jobs for the three or four generations of a beaver family inhabiting a lodge, especially if the dam is a large one. (And they *do* get large: there is a dam half a mile long on the Jefferson River in Montana.) The commitment of labor to this kind of massive project, from cutting the trees to trimming the spillways, makes sense for the beavers only because a dam is meant to last forever. It is not

The beaver will fell this aspen for its branches.

Alert to the nuances of the water's flow, the beaver is always filling a gap here, opening a sluiceway there.

built for one season's usage, as most birds' nests are. Beaver dams are maintained by generation after generation of offspring in the growing colonies. There are dams today that have been in use for more than a century.

Though this stubby, waddling mammal hardly looks like anyone's ideal of an underwater construction engineer, beavers are in fact physically well equipped for their work. The long incisor teeth in the front of their mouths are strong and sharp enough that native Americans in the United States and Canada used them as cutting tools. The fourth finger on the beaver's front paw works as a sort of thumb, allowing the animal to grasp the twigs it hauls and manipulates in the water. With their flat tail for a rudder and their webbed hind feet, beavers swim marvelously; they can hold their breath well, too, staying underwater for as long as fifteen minutes. Their dense fur insulates them against the cold in freezing mountain streams. In fact, beavers inhabit their ponds all through the winter, even when the surface is frozen thick. They nick the dam and let some water flow until a good air space separates the water's surface from the underside of the ice. They breathe in this space, and swim the winter away, eating bark from wood they have stockpiled, often at the bottom of their pools.

Don't try to gnaw trees down unless you have incisors like these!

Note how the full stream above the first beaver dam has become a mere trickle below the fourth. One human dam turns the same trick.

The beaver is widely regarded as the greatest of animal architects, and on the strength of its structures alone, this is easy to understand. The lodges and dams are cleverly designed and well made, from materials difficult to collect and combine into a coherent form. The functional mastery of hydro-engineering is daunting; certainly no other animal structure in the world has to withstand the relentless, elemental pressure borne by a beaver dam spanning a swift river. And these dams and lodges *work*, decade after decade, responding to adjustments, recovering from disasters, holding fast in form and function.

Are Animals Smart?

Even when we are careful to see an animal's actions in terms of its own life, we still notice that many animal qualities are obvious as correlates to our own experiences. We are not mistaken in giving these qualities the same names. We can tell when a cat is suspicious, a bird afraid, a dog lonesome. Why not say so? The mistake may be that we presume in the first place that these are *human* traits crudely mimicked by lesser creatures, and that by sharing our words we are elevating animal behavior above its lowly place. Who is to say humans invented suspiciousness or fear, and that we therefore own its copyright?

Animal structures allow us the same kind of correlation. We can see that a snail shell is like armor, a spiderweb like a fishnet, an ovenbird's nest like a house. But the comparison of things that are *designed* and *made* strikes deeper than does a comparison of feelings. These artifacts lead us to consider whether animals possess the most controversial quality of all, the one we imagine sets us furthest apart from the less-refined, more elemental life of creatures: intelligence.

Most of us would say: People are smart. Animals are . . . well, something else. When a two-year-old human child uses a yardstick to scoop a cookie off a high kitchen counter, we praise the child's native brightness but accept it as a mere step in the development of intellect. But when a bolas spider swings a strand of silk with a sticky globule on the end at a passing insect and hauls the bug in to eat, we treat it more as a bit of luck, an accidental discovery the spider managed, improbably, to repeat and pass on by instinct—a naïve sort of act, far from intellectual. In human history, we are proud of the people of ancient times who made paper: we look back at them as more intelligent than we expected them to be, so far back in time, but we give them a lot of credit for this industrious creativity. Yet show us one of my wasps making paper in the same way—shaving bits of wood, breaking down its cellulose and combining it with chemical agents in the wasp's saliva, then rolling it out into sheets both monochrome and colored—and we treat it as a merely physical capability: Isn't it interesting that the wasp has the mouth and glands to do this? That the Chinese may have learned how to make paper by watching wasps does not make us think any more highly of the insect. *We* are the ones who brought the *brains* to the process. Bravo, humans!

It is true that human intelligence goes far beyond that of insects and birds and amphibians and reptiles and fish and crustaceans and mollusks and our fellow mammals. We have the freedom of improvisation where the animal has the boundary of instinct. We can improvise structures when we need them; with a few exceptions, animals cannot. The ability to im-provise—to create new solutions to immediate problems, to plan innovative strategies without reference to others—is a profoundly individual talent: each one of us can do it because we can think alone. The restrictiveness of instinct is the opposite: it shows that each wasp or panda or octopus is essentially a member of a species that behaves *as a group* in a certain way.

Instincts can be incredibly precise, however. They can guide an animal to the perfect performance over and over of tasks a human would find too exacting in mental and physical concentration and endurance. They can also lead animals to complex actions based on "discoveries" we come upon only through centuries of trial and error. For example, the female praying mantis coats her eggs as she lays them with a viscous liquid, which she immediately whips into a froth with her rear legs; the foam hardens into a tough nut-like shell, with the bubbles trapped inside creating a layered insulation against cold and shock, so the eggs will last through a winter to hatch in the spring. Mantises have been doing this for thousands (if not millions) of years. Yet the "invention" of closed-cell foam insula-

The praying mantis "builds" a closed-cell foam casing for her eggs.

tion—for *human* use, such as in homes and in camping gear—is a recent tribute to the genius of chemical engineers in the plastics industry.

It may be that to appreciate the intelligence of animals we must look at them not as individuals, but as involuntary representatives of the laws of nature. It is no secret that the world follows an underlying orderliness— this is why roses never bloom on chestnut trees, and giraffes never give birth to pandas. We humans have the initiative to move beyond the restrictions of our immediate environment and needs, but animals are much closer to the commandments of nature's law; the orderliness of their actions is not mitigated by the uniquely human ambition to be greater tomorrow than we are today. An animal doesn't care about getting ahead. It cares about staying alive and raising a family: the fundamentals of nature. Accordingly, its wits are clearly focused on these goals, and not beyond.

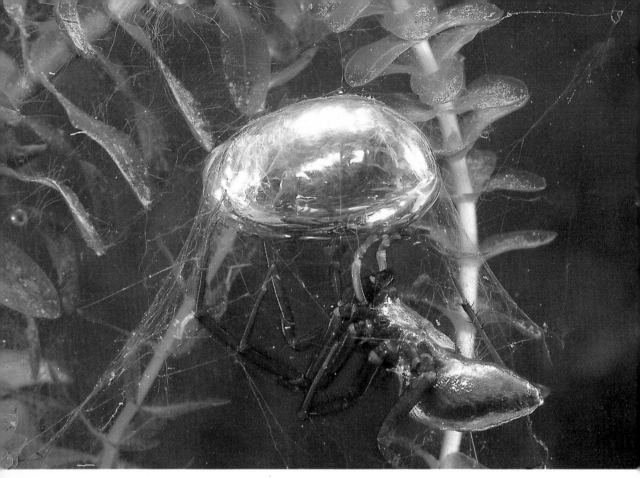

This spider—an air-breathing, terrestrial animal—has built an apartment under-water. First it spun a silk tent on the bottom. Then it filled the roof of the tent with air, making a large bubble of breaths held from trips to the surface. Using this bubble as a reservoir, the spider will hunt fish underwater!

There is perhaps no easier way to appreciate the intelligence of animals, as representing the intricate orderliness of nature, than to study the things they build. When we see birds with stuff in their beaks flying all over the place in the spring, we may be excused for thinking them rather frantic and random. But when we find a few perfectly round baskets of woven grass and a few sacs knitted of reeds, covered with moss, and lined with spider silk, it is hard not to see a system at work. Honeybees in a swarm look as mindless, as clotted with simple instinct, as any group of living things could be. But if they were all to fly back a couple of feet and give us a look at the geometrically exact series of wax hexagons they have been building, very rapidly, with totally efficient cooperation, then their collective bulk suddenly strikes us as complex and involved.

The compass termite mounds boast heating and cooling systems that work as well as those of New York City's Flatiron Building.

Beneath these extended coral polyps grows a great metropolis—a reef, like the one surrounding this turquoise lagoon.

It is true that animal architecture is created primarily according to animal instinct. An individual beaver does not invent the dam, nor does one compass termite decide through personal ingenuity that its two million cronies should erect a flat home following an east–west axis that will catch sunlight on its broad side during cool seasons and skim light off its skinny edges during hot times. These animals are born with blueprints in their consciousness; all of their kind possess the same plans, and together they follow the compulsion to build what they know. It is in the products of this collective clarity of design that we can best appreciate the more elemental kind of intelligence. It is different from studying the personal genius of the architect Frank Lloyd Wright. But fortunately for us, the structures closer to nature reveal their secrets more readily, with a closer connection to needs we can identify, and a beauty that cannot be separated from functions we can witness. Best of all, we can find these architectural marvels all around us, on any stroll through the woods, any walk on the beach.

Glossary

Adaptation—This is the process by which an animal adjusts to conditions that have changed; the animal meets these unexpected demands by using its instincts, intelligence, and physical abilities to find or create what it needs to survive.

Amphibian—This is a class of vertebrate animals that can live in water and on land: frogs, toads, salamanders, newts, and wormlike caecilians. Most amphibians have very simple lungs, as adults, and breathe largely through their moist skin. They are cold-blooded—their body temperature depends on the temperature outside, instead of being regulated from within, as it is in warm-blooded animals. Scientists believe amphibian species used to be fish; millions of years ago their ancestors left the water and, over the course of generations, developed lungs and legs.

Bird—If an animal has feathers, it belongs to this class of vertebrates. Most birds fly and use this gift in all parts of their lives, but some do not; one (the kiwi) does not really even have wings. Birds live very intensely—they are amazingly quick and sensitive, and their hearts beat up to ten times faster than ours do (they are warm-blooded, with a body temperature as much as 12 degrees higher than humans). In North America, we see more of them in the spring and summer because many species fly south to spend the winter in warmer parts of the world (this is called migration).

Crustaceans—These are sometimes called "insects of the sea"; they are in fact in the same large grouping (the arthropods) as insects and spiders. Crustaceans are a primary food for many marine animals and seem to be everywhere in both salt and fresh water. The 26,000 species include many tiny and simple creatures, such as brine shrimp, and more complex animals such as crabs and lobsters. Some of the crabs live on land as well as in water; the wood louse is a crustacean that is entirely terrestrial.

Environment—An environment is the physical surroundings—everything from rocks and air to plants and animals—among which an animal lives. The term is used in two ways. First, scientists define several specific types of environment according to clearly distinct features (for example, salt marsh, old-growth forest, tundra); they try to figure out the very complex relationships between all of the living and non-living things found in that particular kind of place. (In general, they have learned that if one aspect of an environment is changed, even a little, then everything in it is affected. Nothing is unimportant.) Second, all of us—not just scientists—have begun to speak of the environment as the complicated physical wholeness of the earth: the air, water, minerals, and animals among which we must fit.

Evolution—This is a slow, orderly, progressive process through which animals change their physical makeup or behavior, as a means of thriving in a changing world. An evolutionary change takes a long time over many generations of a species (as contrasted with an adaptive change, which can take ten minutes in one individual). In general, animals are always competing—for space, food, and mates with whom they can reproduce their kind. When a certain feature leads one individual to succeed over others (a slightly longer neck that lets it reach higher leaves richer in nutrients; brighter feathers that attract stronger mates; a deeper, more aggressive roar that frightens trespassers; and so on), the animal eats and breeds more vigorously, passing that feature on to its offspring, which in turn succeed, in greater numbers, and pass it on—until the new feature becomes a universal fact of life for that kind of animal.

Fish—These animals are aquatic vertebrates that swim by undulating their bodies, maneuvering with fins. They inhabit the fresh and salt water of all regions, from the polar to the tropical, in a vast range of sizes. To breathe, they extract oxygen from water through gills. Most fish are predators; most lay eggs; and most are covered by scales.

Host—A living thing upon (or inside) which another living thing lives is a host. Sometimes the intruder more or less borrows space, and doesn't especially bother the host; sometimes the intruder steals from the host (or even devours it from the inside) and weakens or kills it.

Insect—This is the largest class of animals in the world: there are about 800,000 known species, and more are being discovered all the time. Insects are invertebrates—they have no skeletons inside. Their adult bodies are divided into three segments (head, thorax, abdomen); they all have six legs, two compound eyes, and a pair of antennae; most have one or two pairs of wings. They live in more places in the world than any other kind of creature, in larger populations. One well-known scientist said to another, "What would life be like if the insects took over the world?" The second scientist laughed and said, "My dear sir, haven't you noticed that they already have?"

Instincts—Animals are born with knowledge about how to live their kind of life. The interior mechanism that supplies this knowledge and puts it into involuntary use is instinct. Instinct gives spiders a mental blueprint for their webs; it makes newly hatched chickens hunker down and peep in terror when a V-shaped shadow passes by them, though they have never seen such a shadow cast by a real hawk (for that matter, neither have they seen what a hawk likes to do to a chicken). When we watch animals, we are amazed at how self-sufficient they are. Instincts are the reason they are able to take such detailed care of themselves, with so little study or instruction. But however exact instincts may be, they do not equip animals to solve unexpected problems with analytical intelligence; instincts are rigid instructions that can only be rigidly applied.

Invertebrates and vertebrates—Vertebrates are animals with backbones; invertebrates are animals without. More than 97 percent of the world's animals are invertebrates. Some of them are basically blobs (amoebas, jellyfish); some are soft but well formed (octopuses, earthworms), some have armored themselves with hard shells that give their bodies a tough definition (coral, lobsters, beetles). Perhaps because humans have backbones, we regard vertebrates as the higher life forms, despite their meager numbers. Mammals, birds, reptiles, amphibians, and fish all have spines; most have internal bony skeletons as well, though some have cartilage instead (sharks), and others have bony plates under the skin (trunkfish) or outside it (turtles).

Larva—Many animals are born with a body quite different from the one they will inhabit when they grow up. They go through one or more changes of shape and eventually attain their maturity. In the early stages the animals are called larvae. Often a larva bears no resemblance to its future form (caterpillar to butterfly, tadpole to frog). Larvae may also live in a different type of environment, follow a different diet, and thrive on a different life-style than the ones they will later settle into.

Mammal—We are pretty familiar with the vertebrate class called mammals; humans belong here, alongside dolphins, dogs, elephants, rats, whales, and lots of other warm-blooded creatures that give birth to living young (except for the oddball platypus and echidna, which lay eggs) and feed them milk. Mammals have one set of replacement teeth, fingernails or claws or hoofs, large brains, and hair. Most mammals walk the land on four legs, though quite a few have adapted to life in the water, some merely showing vestiges of their quadrupedal structure; only one group, the bats, can truly fly, though several other species spread flaps of skin and glide.

Metabolism—An animal's body is essentially a chemistry laboratory in which all reactions are carefully coordinated: somewhere oxygen or sugar is being converted to useful chemicals, somewhere protein or heat is being created. The sum of all chemical activity in the body is called the animal's metabolism.

Metamorphosis—Many animals are born with one body, yet end up with quite another one by the time they become adults. This change of form is called metamorphosis. It can be slow and gradual, or quick and drastic; it can be a complete transformation, or a partial one. The immature and mature forms of a single animal can live in ways that seem to be unrelated—a dragonfly larva that lives underwater and a caterpillar that moseys slowly from leaf to leaf can become dashing aerial insects, and a tadpole capable of nothing but wiggling in water turns into a bounding frog.

Mollusks—These invertebrates live in all parts of the world, land and sea, and cover a range of diversity from the snail to the octopus. They have in common a soft body and, usually, a hard shell (the slug and octopus have lost their hard parts; the squid and cuttlefish retain only vestiges).

Predator—An animal that kills other animals for food is a predator.

Reptile—Snakes, lizards, crocodiles, turtles, and some wormlike things called amphisbaenians make up the class of vertebrates called reptiles. Almost all lay eggs that hatch into babies that look just like the adults (no larval stage). Reptiles are cold-blooded, and most have a scaly, dry skin.

Species—A type of animal that is different from others by reason of physical or geographical distinctions is said to be a species. It's simply a word for the units of individuality in the natural world. Sometimes the distinctions between one species and another are very slight, but generally they follow the animals' own rules of division, mainly expressed in breeding habits: creatures tend to mate within their own species.

Vertebrates—See "Invertebrates."

Acknowledgments
and Photo Credits

The Knowing Nature Books are inspired by the broad spirit of inquiry and richness of detail in the *Nature* television series. The books are original works, however, and their material is not derived from the *Nature* programs. Thanks to those who make the *Nature* series possible: George Page and David Heeley at Thirteen/WNET, New York, with the generous support of the American Gas Association, Siemens, and Canon.

Personal thanks to the people who have helped make the book: David Wolff, Lee Anne Martin, Margaret Ferguson, Elaine Chubb, David Reisman, and Licia Hurst.

Cover photo is a dew-draped orb; photo on title page, honey in comb; photo on page 2, paper wasp nest; photo on page 10, Atlantic lobster; photo on page 26, common mole; photo on page 40, masked weaverbird; photo on page 56, gorilla.

Cover © E. R. Degginger / Animals Animals
Title © Donald Specker / Animals Animals
PAGE
2 © Ken Lewis / Animals Animals
5 © Raymond Mendez / Animals Animals
6 © Kirtley Perkins, National Audubon Society Collection / Photo Researchers
8 © Michael P. Gadomski, National Audubon Society Collection / Photo Researchers
10 © E. R. Degginger / Animals Animals
12 © Scott Johnson / Animals Animals
13 (top) © Dr. Paul A. Zahl, National Audubon Society Collection / Photo Researchers

8   © Michael P. Gadomski, National Audubon Society Collection / Photo Researchers

10   © E. R. Degginger / Animals Animals

12   © Scott Johnson / Animals Animals

13 (top)   © Dr. Paul A. Zahl, National Audubon Society Collection / Photo Researchers.

13 (bottom)   © Jerome Wexler / Photo Researchers

15   © Tom McHugh, Steinhart Aquarium / Photo Researchers

16   © Dr. Paul A. Zahl, National Audubon Society Collection / Photo Researchers

17   © Oxford Scientific Films / Animals Animals

18   © E. R. Degginger / Animals Animals

20   © Bill Bachman, National Audubon Society Collection / Photo Researchers

23   © Donald Specker / Animals Animals

24   © Scott Camazine, National Audubon Society Collection / Photo Researchers

25   © Carol Hughes / Bruce Coleman, Inc.

26   © Leonard Lee Rue III, National Audubon Society Collection / Photo Researchers

28   © Mike Neumann, National Audubon Society Collection / Photo Researchers

29   © Animals Animals

33   © Gary Retherford, National Audubon Society Collection / Photo Researchers

34   © Philip K. Sharpe, Oxford Scientific Films / Animals Animals

35 (top)   © S. J. Krasemann, National Audubon Society Collection / Photo Researchers

35 (bottom)   © Don Getsug / Photo Researchers

36   © François Gohier, National Audubon Society Collection / Photo Researchers

37   © Tom McHugh, National Museum of Natural History / Photo Researchers

38   © Mary M. Thacher, National Audubon Society Collection / Photo Researchers

40   © G. I. Bernard, Oxford Scientific Films / Animals Animals

42   © Rexford Lord, National Audubon Society Collection / Photo Researchers

43   © Tom McHugh, National Audubon Society Collection / Photo Researchers

45   © R. H. Armstrong / Animals Animals

46   © Steve Maslowski, National Audubon Society Collection / Photo Researchers

47 (top)   © Kenneth W. Fink, National Audubon Society Collection / Photo Researchers

47 (bottom)   © Margot Conte / Animals Animals

48   © Mantis Wildlife Films, Oxford Scientific Films / Animals Animals

50   © Pat & Tom Leeson, National Audubon Society Collection / Photo Researchers

52   © Gregory K. Scott, National Audubon Society Collection / Photo Researchers

53   © Stephen J. Krasemann, National Audubon Society Collection / Photo Researchers

54 (top)   © Kenneth W. Fink, National Audubon Society Collection / Photo Researchers

54 (bottom)   © Betty Derig / Photo Researchers

56   © Peter B. Kaplan, National Audubon Society Collection / Photo Researchers

59   © Maria Zorn / Animals Animals

60   © Oxford Scientific Films / Animals Animals

61 (top)   © Bill Bachman, National Audubon Society Collection / Photo Researchers

61 (bottom)   © Joseph P. Sinnott

62 (top)   © Andrew J. Martinez, National Audubon Society Collection / Photo Researchers

62 (bottom)   © Douglas Faulkner, National Audubon Society Collection / Photo Researchers

Index